WORD PLAY

WHERE WORDS

Washington, D.C.

U.S. Capitol

street

by Carrie B. Sheely

PEBBLE
a capstone imprint

Take a trip to a park.
Then stop at the ice cream shop and go home.

Where else can you go? Follow along and let words tell you!

park

playground

ice cream shop

grocery
store

supermarket

mall stores

shopping mall

shopping center

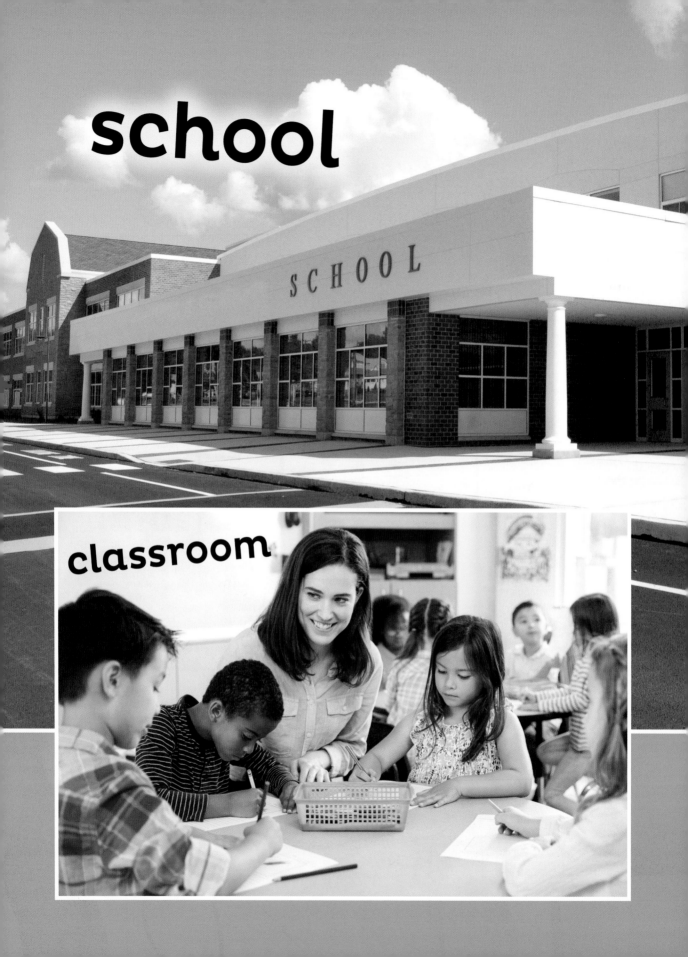

school

classroom

library

Wrigley Field

ballpark

Chicago

stadium

What other places do you see?

Times Square

street

New York City

ZOO

aquarium

marine
animal
park

Antarctica

ocean

South Pole

Grand Canyon

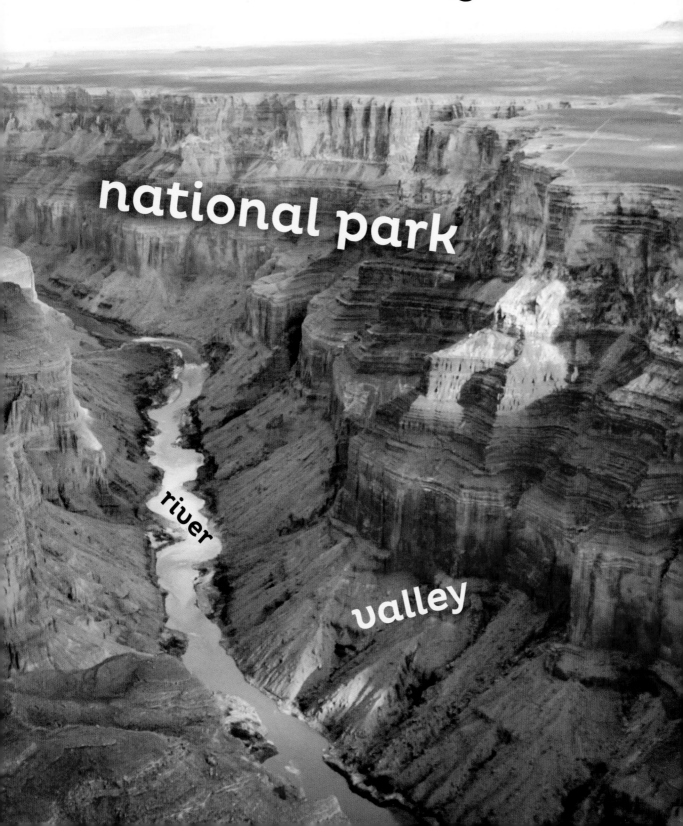

national park

river

valley

houses

homes

house

forest

lake

Neuschwanstein Castle

sun

space

moon

Earth

beach

Coney Island

apartment buildings

amusement park

farm

barn

pasture

jungle

rain
forest

victory lane

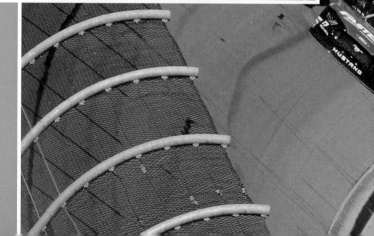

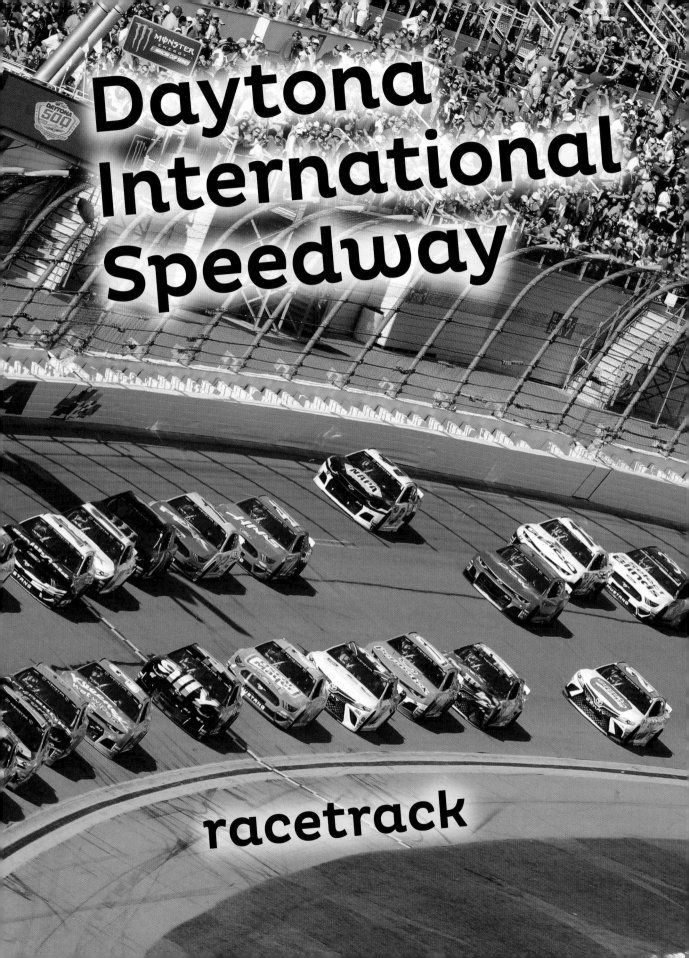

Daytona International Speedway

racetrack

fire station

firehouse

police station

apple orchard

mountains

path

trail

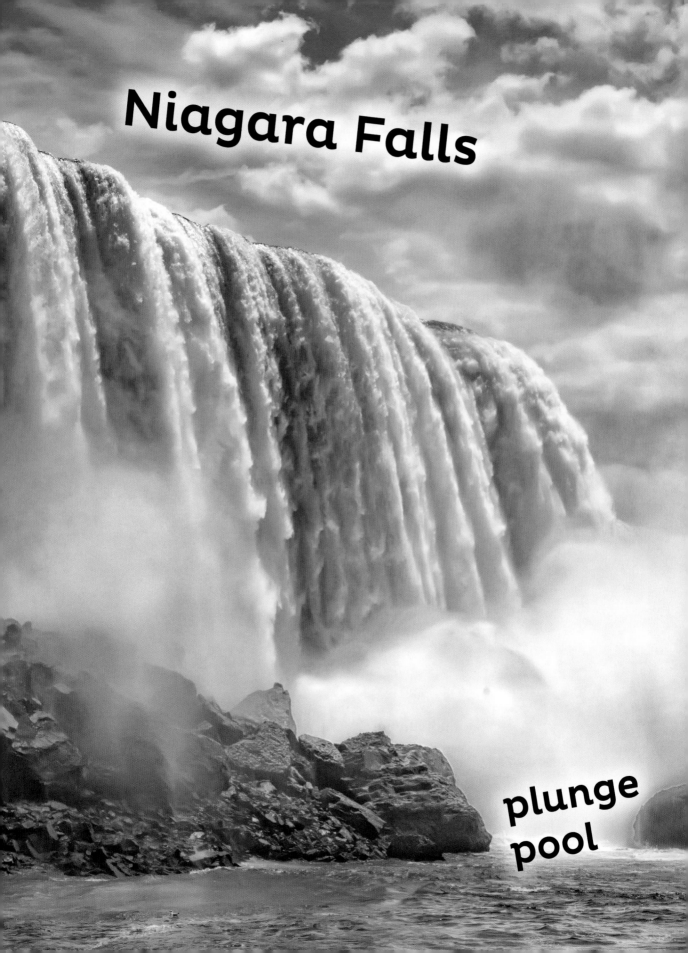

Niagara Falls

plunge pool

Giza Pyramid Complex

Sahara Desert

Pebble Sprout is published by Pebble,
an imprint of Capstone.
1710 Roe Crest Drive
North Mankato, Minnesota 56003
www.capstonepub.com

**Library of Congress Cataloging-in-Publication Data
is available on the Library of Congress website.**
ISBN: 978-1-9771-1310-8 (library binding)
ISBN: 978-1-9771-1826-4 (paperback)
ISBN: 978-1-9771-1316-0 (eBook PDF)

Summary: With engaging photos,
introduces nouns that name places.

Image Credits
Dreamstime: Napat Chaichanasiri, 2; iStockphoto: andresr,
3, FangXiaNuo, 7; Shutterstock: Action Sports Photography,
24, 24–25, Amineah, 14–15, Aphelleon, 18-19, Cynthia
Farmer, 6 (top), Elenarts, 16, Evdoha_spb, 30, FamVeld,
28, Frank Romeo, 8–9, Joseph Sohm, 14, Julia Kuznetsova,
29, Kamira, 20–21, KPG_Payless, 17, Laborant, 5, Luciano
Mortula LGM, 10–11, Manuel Esteban, 26–27, Mike Liu, 13,
Monkey Business Images, 4, 6 (bottom), Orhan Cam, 1, Petr
Hruza, 27 (bottom), sculpies, 31, Sean Pavone, cover, Sergey
Uryadnikov, 23, Sunychka Sol, 12, V J Matthew, 22

Editorial Credits
Designer: Juliette Peters
Media Researcher: Svetlana Zhurkin
Production Specialist: Katy LaVigne

Printed and bound in the USA.
PA99

Titles in this set:

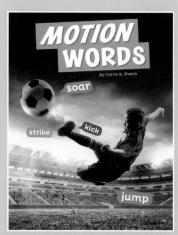

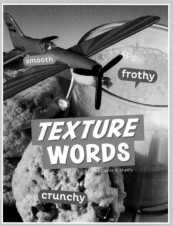

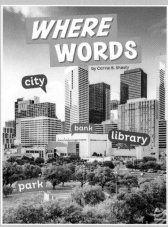